Death

by

Manning Goodwin

First published 2021 by The Hedgehog Poetry Press

Published in the UK by
The Hedgehog Poetry Press
5, Coppack House
Churchill Avenue
Clevedon
BS21 6QW

www.hedgehogpress.co.uk

ISBN: 978-1-913499-52-5

Copyright © Manning Goodwin 2021

The right of Manning Goodwin to be identified as the author of this work has been asserted in accordance with the Copyright, Designs and Patents Act 1988.

All rights reserved. No part of this publication may be reproduced, stored in or introduced into a retrieval system, or transmitted in any form, or by any means (electronic, mechanical, photocopying, recording or otherwise) without prior written permissions of the publisher. Any person who does any unauthorised act in relation to this publication may be liable for criminal prosecution and civil claims for damages.

9 8 7 6 5 4 3 2 1

A CIP Catalogue record for this book is available from the British Library.

Contents

Falling Petals 5
At End of Day 6
Good Friday 7
Concerning Poison and Ways to Die 8
The Last of Days 9
Sockeye Salmon 10
Dichotomies 12
Each End is a Beginning 13
Consequence and Consecration 14
Choice 15
Bitter End 16
At End of Life on Earth 17

FALLING PETALS

Memories of missing people drag,
distract our thoughts to vapor trails;
loved ones we've known who now move on.

Elsewhere they go, leave us in dark,
they are petals dropped onto water:
some sink, while others sail away.

Did petals fall from tree blossoms,
or from where now live parted ones?

AT END OF DAY

I read aloud my favourite good book
on this my final day of earth's journey.
Thank all those who accompany me here
for all the poetry and love they've given.
It's been a hard but rich and fruitful time.
I've learned to trust the one who leads my way
to even feel the calm of others' striving.
I love my wife and family, I'm blessed.

GOOD FRIDAY

Two chaps with caps came by all dressed in black.
Were they Death's squad replete with sunny smiles?
Named James and Simon, able blokes, and willing.
"Is my time up?" I asked, prepared, to die.
They laughed: "Oh No! Wood chips – too big they were,
and blocked the boiler system until Tuesday –
so please shut down your heat from now to then."
They took away my flame, yet let me live.

CONCERNING POISON AND WAYS TO DIE

On belladonna plant four leaves form cross;
they slowly wilt as berries first mature,
shiny blue-black, tempting your wish to pick,
but if you pluck and eat, you will be dead.
Women can squeeze modest amounts to make
their eyes large and attractive, dark – for men,
who's self-possession, faced with beauty, wanders.
Socrates stood accused of youth's corruption,
with death as penalty, but took response:
he drank a draught of hemlock to cause self death.
Cicero fled, and when, in flight from soldiers
sent by Octavian, they'd captured him –
he seized the sword and gored himself.
Octavian lost his office late in life –
for him depressing sorrow; but then his wife
injected poison in low-flying figs
that hung on garden tree, where he would pick.
He ate – perhaps half knowing – thus he died.
When heart stops still, doctors use belladonna,
to jolt response to blood's reviving pulse.
Deplored's a death by self – poisons aren't tasty –
medicines encroach on sense of purpose.
There's ever tasks to do and grounds to live;
first off: if heart won't work, love can't flow.

THE LAST OF DAYS

When growing old – it comes to all –
we're bedded, pillowed, searching pastimes,
seeking day-long fascination,
challenge, richest int'rest, meaning,
reading books and hearing music,
writing poems, working iPads.
Receptive can we feel to visits,
wife too – all wait for strikes of lightning.

SOCKEYE SALMON

How long we've sought to be good fish,
doing the task that Thou, Oh God,
have predetermined for our race.
The shallow stream I swim to source
to find the place whence fathers came
and where I'll spawn for year that comes
the Sockeye salmon for your Pacific,
fulfilled each year, renewing cycles.

We did not know, held there within the rock,
you'd sealed the mineral gold from eons past,
stored out of sight to both our race and man.
What purpose was this lode long destined for?
Why now have you graced man, allowed discovery?
You know how man will greed for such commodity,
how he will hoard, and buy a useless luxury,
disturb world currencies and speculate.

Miners will come, strip mine of gold,
settle down, build process plants,
poison stream, disturb our lives.
So soon our race will die, right out.
Families downstream who've lived
generations fishing, will lose
their work and homes and be no more,
not to come back when gold is gone.

Oh God, what purpose this command, creation?
You could have seen the conflict long ago.
Oh why inflict such dire deed and doom,
not hint where lies a moral, right outcome?
Or is there some grand plan of evolution,
which yet to those on earth seems so inscrutable,
of which your angels sing in daily choirs?
We swish our tails and flash our light-filled colors.

We jump the falls that thunder down.
We feed both bear and man, surviving.
And now, Oh God, you make man choose,
whose soul has made but modest steps.
The gold is outer ore of matter,
some lives have worked the gold within.
For Thee, Oh God, I'd be both fish and poet;
pray grace our poem with peace and joy.

DICHOTOMIES

Says Homeopathy's initiator:
"The same heals same" – so, chemo zaps the cancer.
As evil zaps evil? But hate breeds hate.
Hate is redeemed when heart opens with love.
The doc's report: "Treatment achieves remission,"
we feel the winter spring to celebration.
Leaves lost, we see hawthorn's red globes hang out –
the nest of last year's spring, like corpse revived
for use again next year; we transform age,
achieving inward deeds that suit our years.
And as in some death lodge, we end prepare,
or life's next step, but full-infused with light
to make our nature new and sun more bright.
And round we go to those we've hurt for years
to ask forgiveness, thank for all they've done,
accept where grudge is held, and bless instead.

EACH END IS A BEGINNING

He sensed impending death, urged she not lament:
"Firebird, you celebrate freedom's fortune".
At the advent of love's most awful altar,
dancing on the heartstrings of your lover,
you see his carcass drip it's fate into the flame.
You know his Spirit's gone to eternal glory.

CONSEQUENCE AND CONSECRATION

The future King of France wishes to wed
a lass who hails from overseas: l'Americaine.
My wife would like to feed the camels;
her gorging friend will fill on salmon smoked;
I would prefer to ply in words this poem.
Who's to say which work is most important.
Let each complete the task that suits them best;
each left to own pursuit shall find their fruit.
Fix not salvation's shape: its threads feel fragile.
Beware, while camel-wife-friend, exalted King,
exult, French river salmon go extinct.
How can we keep the New World would-be queen
alive and here in France with finer fodder,
devoting self to serve the King's intentions?
Misdated Tombstone

I slipped up once again by chance
when tombstone planning: I wrote
a five instead of twenty-five
thus lopping off a score of years.

The rump of life at seventy-four,
despite the countless fits and starts,
the num'rous failures, spurts, assays,
were thronged with gold and gifts so rich.

So true I wrote, "From stars begot,
and back to stars he goes again".
Here lies the body's ash in peace;
a joyous soul, life's venture shon upon.

CHOICE

Fast driving as a lifetime habit requires
hubris or recompense at untimely moment,
not least because your mate's best intentioned orders
would have you drive in lane, more slow, with care.
It's true - attention lapse and quick response
become with age of ever more concern,
but nerves frazzle with fears bemoaned unbridled.
When the eventual crash transpires - you'll join in death,
foreshadowed by Sebald, Fuller and Lusseyran.
Is cause then payback for a careless life,
for heart unopened to all love and care,
or is the time for soul's embrace a cosmic choice?

BITTER END

Fathers will all to fatherhood be tamed –
hearing of son's own death, they're shocked and lamed.
Pressed into inward heart, centered in ache
within the circling arms of care and loss.

When youth first broached the dangerous trip beyond,
it was to swim in China's Sea of sharks,
or race the Afghan's pony out of breath,
or be the poison-darted pygmy's brother.

Lips purse the blessing, gilded palm withheld,
the youth's resolve, lofted on wings of justice,
strikes freedom's bell for self and leaves the home.
Father will pay the wage in heaven's coin.0

AT END OF LIFE ON EARTH

A fight from four bronchitis weeks of illness
to warmth and dryness found in Lanzarote
chasing away the cough, congestion, gloom.
Regime follows of writing, reads and walks.
Now freedom's joy reigns black volcanic land
with sunny days and vibrant mountain sunsets,
delicious food without our kitchen duties,
time to deliberate, choose life's next tasks.
Back home, files and books must be relinquished,
but ninety years soon comes and ninety one's
thirteen times seven shows me at the brink.
My wife and I must reckon death will knock,
but first we'll help, then learn to stand alone,
becoming clear how Christ has shaped our lives,
resolving then if karma's task's complete,
then finding peace, before our work in heaven.

ACKNOWLEDGEMENTS

With Many thanks to Louise Cronin for help in preparing these poems for publication.

Thanks also to friends in our monthly meeting of the group Poetry Exchange.

And many accolades should go also go to Mark Davidson for his challenges and competitions, fostering members to produce their best poems , as well as his tireless work in publishing their poems.

The sculpture featured on the cover artwork is © Manning Goodwin.

To find out more about Manning, his writing and artwork, visit his web site:

www.manninggoodwin.com

www.ingramcontent.com/pod-product-compliance
Lightning Source LLC
Chambersburg PA
CBHW021455080526
44588CB00009B/867